WHAT EVERY TE[...]

Living the Faith

Developed by the
Christian Education Staff
of The General Board of Discipleship
of The United Methodist Church

DISCIPLESHIP RESOURCES

P.O. BOX 340003 • NASHVILLE, TN 37203-0003
www.discipleshipresources.org

This booklet was developed by the Christian Education Staff of the General Board of Discipleship of The United Methodist Church. It is one in a series of booklets designed to provide essential knowledge for teachers. Members of the staff who helped write and develop this series are Terry Carty, Bill Crenshaw, Donna Gaither, Rick Gentzler, Mary Alice Gran, Susan Hay, Betsey Heavner, Diana Hynson, Carol Krau, MaryJane Pierce Norton, Deb Smith, Julia Wallace, and Linda Whited.

Reprinted 2002, 2003

Cover and book design by Joey McNair
Cover illustration by Mike Drake

Edited by Debra D. Smith and Cindy S. Harris

ISBN 0-88177-365-4

Scripture quotations, unless otherwise indicated, are from the New Revised Standard Version of the Bible, copyright © 1989 by the Division of Christian Education of the National Council of the Churches of Christ in the USA. All rights reserved. Used by permission.

WHAT EVERY TEACHER NEEDS TO KNOW ABOUT LIVING THE FAITH. Copyright © 2002 Discipleship Resources. All rights reserved. No part of this book may be reproduced in any form whatsoever, print or electronic, without written permission, except in the case of brief quotations embodied in critical articles or reviews. For information regarding rights and permissions, contact Discipleship Resources, P.O. Box 340003, Nashville, TN 37203-0003; phone 800-814-7833 (toll-free) or 615-340-7068; fax 615-340-1789; e-mail mgregory@gbod.org.

DR365

Contents

Introduction 5

The Power of Influence 9

The Power of Actions. 15

The Power of Authority 19

The Power of Caring 23

The Power of Curriculum. 29

The Power of Listening 33

The Power of Touch. 37

The Power of Words 41

Going Further 45

Helpful Resources 47

*This book is dedicated to
YOU,
a teacher of
children, youth, or adults,
WHO,
with fear, excitement, joy,
and commitment,
allows God to lead you
in the call to
TEACH.*

*The gifts he gave were that some would be . . .
teachers, . . . for building up the body of Christ.
(Ephesians 4:11-12)*

Introduction

In accepting the invitation to teach in your congregation, you have entered into a time of growing as a Christian while you lead others in growing along with you. Whether you are a teacher of children, youth, or adults, the way you live out your Christian faith is a significant witness to those you teach.

The role of teacher carries with it a great deal of power—and the responsibility to use that power ethically and in a way that affirms the members of your class as beloved children of God. This booklet describes eight areas of power that teachers have. This power can be used for good, or in ways that hurt people and contradict God's good news. It can be used to control people, or to enhance learning.

As teachers we have the responsibility of learning about the power we have and then choosing how we will use the power. The abuse of power occurs when we use power to gratify our own desires rather than to carry out God's sacred trust. It happens when we refuse to own the responsibility that comes with the privilege of power. Choosing to use this power for good and then developing daily practices to increase our skill will develop our personal spiritual life. As our faith grows and we become more obedient to using the power we have for good in the world, we will become more effective teachers and role models for others, as Jesus' life is a model for us.

Teachers and small-group leaders are growing in faith. As teachers we pay attention to our relationships with God and with others. We seek to live our faith in our daily lives. We create safe, healthy settings for people to seek God, respond to God's grace, and find support and encouragement for living as disciples in the world.

Growing in faith, which helps us become spiritual leaders, is a life-changing experience that continues throughout life. We do not grow in faith alone. We grow with the help of God; and we grow with the help of our congregation, who supports us by providing opportunities for learning, resources for teaching, prayer, and training.

This booklet is one of ten that will equip you for teaching. Use the entire series to reinforce your knowledge, skills, and abilities.

Other booklets in this series are
What Every Teacher Needs to Know About
- *the Bible*
- *Christian Heritage*
- *Classroom Environment*
- *Curriculum*
- *Faith Language*
- *People*
- *Teaching*
- *Theology*
- *The United Methodist Church*

The Power of Influence

Who was your favorite teacher? A newspaper columnist recently asked readers to briefly describe a favorite teacher. Who would you nominate? Think about all the teachers you have had. Whom do you remember? What teacher has been influential in your life? What do you remember about that teacher? What is the impact your favorite teacher had on your life?

When responses to the newspaper columnist's question began to appear in the newspaper column, there was an interesting trend. The stories described teachers who had made the students feel loved and valued. Some people wrote about their first teacher, or a junior high teacher, or a teacher from their young-adult years. There were stories about teachers who listened to students when they had problems, teachers who spent extra time to help students pass a test, teachers who helped students discover their vocation, and teachers who inspired students with a love of learning. No one wrote about a particular lesson or teaching method. No one wrote about specific curriculum they remembered. They wrote about people who had influenced their lives.

The Model of Jesus

In God's world, people are more important than facts or methods or curriculum. Who you are as a teacher is of primary importance. Your faith in God and love of all God's people will have the greatest influence on students. This is true whether you teach children, youth, or adults. When asked,

> "Which commandment is the first of all?" Jesus answered, "The first is, 'Hear, O Israel: the Lord our God, the Lord is one; you shall love the Lord your God with all your heart, and with all your soul, and with all your mind, and with all your strength.' The second is this, 'You shall love your neighbor as yourself.'"
> (Mark 12:28-31a)

Jesus' Great Commandment must inform all that teachers say and do. Jesus' life shows us how to live this way. Jesus lived in a rhythm of prayerful attentiveness to God for guidance, and alert awareness of the people and places he encountered in his life. Jesus lived in right relationship with God and people. His human life is a model for teaching that still influences people two thousand years later.

Your Role

Many beginning teachers feel insecure about the knowledge and teaching skills they think they lack. While it is important for teachers to prepare by increasing knowledge, learning teaching skills, and planning, even beginning teachers must consider the great influence they have just by being in the teaching role. Teachers throughout history have been respected as influential leaders in communities and cultures. All who have the role of teacher have influential power.

The influence of role models is powerful and often occurs unconsciously. While our actions, both conscious and unconscious, may be based on our own experience, knowledge, culture, and even economic and social situation, we need to remember that God has given humans the ability to make choices about our words and actions. Our choices can add to or subtract from good in the world. Teachers need to think about the power they have and take seriously the responsibility to use their power thoughtfully and wisely.

Our United Methodist heritage provides a guideline for teachers in their relationships with students. Around 1739, John Wesley established the General Rules for all who met together to grow in faith. This set of guidelines continues to provide guidance for modern-day United Methodists. The General Rules can be found on pages 71–74 of *The Book of Discipline of The United Methodist Church—2000* (The United Methodist Publishing House, 2000). The first of the General Rules states that we should do no harm. As you read this booklet, reflect on the actions that do no harm to the spiritual, mental, emotional, and physical health of your students.

Spiritual Exercise

Think about a teacher who was significant in your life. In what ways did that teacher influence you? Write a short prayer asking God to help you use your power of influence in ways that honor God and respect the worth of each class member. Pray this prayer before each class.

The Power of Actions

My friend Donna greets everyone she meets with a smile. She gives of herself and her resources beyond measure. Donna is a wonderful baker and a good cook. Neighbors, newcomers, teenagers, and elderly homebound folk all enjoy what Donna provides. Along with food for the body, Donna always speaks a word of encouragement and hope for the soul. One day when I asked Donna about her positive actions and attitude, she told me a story:

> When I was a small child, we often spent time with cousins. I was one of the older children in the extended family, and my mother often told me to watch carefully for the "shadows" who were watching me. She meant the younger cousins who watched to see what I did. My mother was a kind and generous woman, loved by all the people we knew, and I wanted to be

like her. I took her advice seriously and developed a keen awareness that anywhere I am, a "shadow" will see what I do.

Communication specialists tell us that the most powerful form of communication is our nonverbal actions. Powerful emotions like love, compassion, and hatred are communicated strongly through actions. We know how true this is with babies, with people who are ill, and with people whom society marginalizes. We often forget this power when we teach able-bodied people who seem similar to us. But our nonverbal response to our students has an impact on their lives and on the lives of any other "shadows" who are watching and learning.

Donna takes seriously the power that her actions have to influence others. People disregard or abuse this power when their words and actions do not match. When a teacher says, "I'll call you this week," the teacher must make sure to follow through. Integrity means that a person's words and actions match! A teacher who has integrity not only tells of God's love but also acts in ways that make that love evident.

Doing Good

The first of the General Rules established by John Wesley is to do no harm. The second is to do good. The purpose of doing good is not to earn God's approval. Rather, when we engage in acts of compassion, mercy, and justice, we allow God to be active in our lives. These actions become channels through which we can receive God's love. Wesley referred to such channels as means of grace.

Church school teachers communicate a message of God's love through their actions as they greet students, remember the missing students, follow up on the joys and concerns expressed by students, respond to hard questions, and handle classroom discipline.

Teachers must teach and model "holy habits," that is, ways of living that bring one ever closer to God and God's creation. Teachers are not called to be perfect and without sin, but for their students they are role models of how to embody Christian living.

Of course, the power of action extends beyond the classroom. As you are involved in mission and ministry outside the walls of the church, you create new opportunities for God to work in your life, and you model to your students that living the faith encompasses all of life.

Spiritual Exercise

Read Matthew 25:34-40 slowly, with attentiveness to your reaction to the words. When a particular word or phrase seems important to you, close your eyes and repeat that word or phrase quietly. Ask God to show you how you can live this Scripture today. At the end of the day read the Scripture again. Ask God to bring to your mind actions of your day that have been pleasing to God. Wait silently and expectantly. Then thank God for being with you during the day, and ask God to guide your actions tomorrow.

The Power of Authority

From everyone to whom much has been given, much will be required; and from the one to whom much has been entrusted, even more will be demanded.

(Luke 12:48)

My first teaching assignment was a public school in the rural South. I worked hard to prepare each day and tried to learn the accents and customs that were new and seemed strange to me. I was nervous on the first day of parent-teacher conferences. I had asked the other teachers for advice. I did what I could to make the classroom and my youthful self look professional for the first meeting with my students' parents. The first couple was a farmer in denim bib overalls and his farm wife in a clean but faded dress. They came in shyly and hung on every word I spoke about their daughter. They didn't have any questions but told me I was to do whatever I needed to do to make her learn. Suddenly it occurred to me that they were as nervous as I was! I was so surprised. I didn't have parenting experience; I didn't even feel confident about my teaching skill.

I learned how powerful the role of teacher is. In spite of my personal insecurity, I was in the role of teacher! This couple, all the parents, the community, and my students had expectations and impressions based on the authority of the role of teacher.

Think back to your own experience as a child. Do you remember believing that whatever your teacher said had to be right, because the teacher had said it? The authority of the teacher is not limited to just teachers of children. Even if you have been a member of an adult class for years, when you assume the role of teacher your words are almost always respected as more authoritative.

Using Your Authority

As you accept the role of teacher in the church, you step into the role of all teachers before you. The greatest teacher, Jesus, forms people's expectations and perceptions. You use your authority appropriately when you create a learning environment that is spiritually, emotionally, psychologically, and physically safe for each student.

For example, a preschool teacher who believes that people should not hit or bite one another uses words and actions to help students learn to verbalize their needs. The teacher knows the church's policies related to discipline and has decided the consequence of hitting and biting before the class starts. If the teacher responds to a student who hits or bites by hitting or biting the student, the teacher is abusing his or her authority! When a teacher responds by hitting or biting, students learn that one with more power and authority can use that power and authority to control smaller and weaker people.

Whether the rules for your class are formal or informal, whether they are set by you or by the class, you must be prepared to follow through with appropriate enforcement. Recall again the General Rule from John Wesley to do no harm. The abuse of authority can cause great harm. Think carefully about how you are using the authority that has been entrusted to you.

Spiritual Exercise

Meditate on Paul's words to the Romans in chapters 12 and 13, especially in Romans 13:1: "There is no authority except from God." The role of teacher carries a certain authority, an authority that allows you to be listened to as soon as you start teaching. Teaching authority increases in one who humbly yet firmly loves and serves others, showing them how to live.

The Power of Caring

Come to me, all you that are weary and are carrying heavy burdens, and I will give you rest. . . . I am gentle and humble in heart, and you will find rest for your souls.

(Matthew 11:28, 29)

Tom came to the church youth group when he finished the sixth grade. He was big for a twelve-year-old, and his size gave him an extra measure of awkwardness as he sauntered in. He had a hard time with academics and a history of being in the principal's office for bullying. He had a reputation as a troublemaker from elementary church school classes, a reputation created from his reaction to years of teasing from others. The youth group sponsors were expecting Tom and had determined to offer him a fresh start.

This particular group of youth sponsors had worked together for two years and were a strong team committed to creating true hospitality for young people as they made the hard journey from childhood to adulthood. They planned and prayed together. They understood the need for firm love for each youth in the group. They understood the power of caring and the abuse that comes from trying to control others. They understood that they could not make Tom do anything, but that they could care for him. They were committed to creating a space where Tom and the others would be safe and feel enough trust to ask questions.

It was a tough year—even tougher than seventh grade is for every youth. Tom couldn't escape his school reputation, and he showed up each Sunday battered from his week in the world. The other seventh graders were not able to stand against peer pressure to be his friends at school. However, the youth sponsors reminded themselves, Tom was still coming on Sundays. Tom was finding something to sustain him on Sundays.

In the eighth grade, Tom started to bring his friends to the youth group. Tom's friends had never been to church before. They partied hard on Saturday night, smoked in the alley behind the church before youth group, and used language never before heard in church. The youth sponsors continued their firm love and caring for each one who came.

Then Tom's friends started coming to church on Sunday morning! Good church people began to question the youth sponsors. Within six months, Tom and his friends stopped regular attendance at the church. The pressure was just too uncomfortable. The youth director made occasional phone calls and was available when calls came from Tom in the middle of the night.

When Tom was twenty years old, he stopped by to see his friend the youth director. Tom was almost as awkward as he had been in the seventh grade, but now he had a regular job. He proudly brought his daughter to meet his friend. Life is still hard for Tom, but he is a strong witness to the power of caring.

True caring does not try to force or control another; caring does not shame or bully a student, whether the student is two years old, or twelve, or thirty-five, or ninety.

The Ways You Care

Caring is usually not demonstrated in a one-time, extraordinary manner. It is more often shown in the consistent small acts of compassion and concern that continually remind the people in your class that they are not alone. Sometimes what seems like an insignificant word or action provides the bit of grace that enables a person to envision a hopeful future.

Think about the class you teach. In what ways do you care for the members of your class? In what ways do they care for one another? How does the class care for you?

The Power of Prayer

One of the most significant ways you can care for the members of your class is to pray for them and to provide opportunities for class members to pray for one another. No matter what age a person is, knowing that someone else is praying for him or her provides comfort and strength.

Spiritual Exercise

Read Mark 4:36-41, especially noticing verse 38. There are two remarkable things about verse 38. First, Jesus was asleep during the storm, content that God was caring for him. Second, Jesus' followers challenged whether he cared for them. As you reflect on the story about Tom and the story about the disciples, what do you learn about caring for your students?

The Power of Curriculum

The Lord judges the peoples;
judge me, O Lord, according to my
righteousness
and according to the integrity that is
in me.

(Psalm 7:8)

Curriculum is sometimes described as the interaction of class members with the content of the faith, materials, resources, and one another. Age-appropriate printed curriculum resources geared to the interests of students provide the content for a well-rounded Christian education.

Part of the curriculum is the unspoken culture of a classroom. A warm, welcoming teaching space where all students are appreciated and valued is a powerful statement conveyed without words. This is a positive use of curriculum.

On the other hand, a classroom that has an unspoken rule that declares, "It is better to be nice than honest," creates an environment where people are not willing to risk asking tough questions. When spirituality is used to judge others, when words and actions in a classroom tear down one person in order to build another up, and when shame is used to get someone to agree, then spiritual abuse is occurring. Allowing an atmosphere in which such statements and feelings are part of the curriculum is a misuse of the power of curriculum.

Another part of the curriculum is the knowledge and experience of people in the group. A teacher with self-confidence to share the teaching role can invite others to bring their knowledge and experience to enhance the lesson. For example, a class member who has traveled to the Middle East can bring insight that illuminates the content of Bible passages. However, singular experience and specialized knowledge can be misused when it attempts to control people. For example, knowledge from a particular trip by one person can be presented with an air of superiority that discourages questions.

It is important for teachers to help students apply the content of each lesson to their daily lives. Finding meaning in life empowers people to share their faith with others and to learn more about faith and life.

Spiritual Exercise

Read Matthew 7:24-28. Students have some responsibility for applying the lesson; teachers have responsibility for presenting useful and appropriate lessons; but only God can transform lives. Reflect on the difference between hearing (or reading) the words of a lesson and having the lesson transform a student's life.

The Power of Listening

After listening to Job and his friends speak for over thirty chapters, we hear a younger man, Elihu, cry out,

> Therefore I say, "Listen to me;
> let me also declare my opinion."
> (Job 32:10)

All of us have probably felt like Elihu at times. The need to be listened to runs deep in our souls.

On the surface, listening appears to be a passive act; but in reality a good listener is highly involved in the communication process. As you listen to someone, you are not just listening for information. You are listening for the feelings, hopes, and dreams that the other person is revealing. You become a safe companion as the person explores new ideas or reevaluates previously held beliefs. Listening is a holy endeavor.

When you listen carefully to another person, you communicate that you value the person. This kind of deep listening conveys understanding so that the other is empowered to grow and learn. As a teacher, you have the opportunity not only to listen to the members of your class but also to help them listen to one another.

Because we can listen faster than we can speak, we are sometimes tempted to fill our listening time by thinking about how we intend to respond rather than by concentrating on what the other person is saying. We may appear to be listening but are actually holding a debate in our mind. When we do this, we are abusing the holy task of listening.

Keys to Listening

- Listen not only for facts but for the feelings behind the facts.
- Give the person speaking the gift of a nonjudgmental presence.
- Don't interrupt or jump in with a comment when the person pauses.
- Avoid jumping to conclusions about how the person is feeling or what the person is thinking.
- Look at the person as you listen to him or her. What the person is saying with his or her body language is as important as what he or she is saying with his or her voice. Listen with your eyes as well as your ears.
- When listening to a child, move to the same physical level as the child. This may mean that you need to sit on the floor or kneel.
- Don't try to solve the problems of the person you are listening to. Your role is to listen, not to fix.

Spiritual Exercise

Read Romans 14:13. Reflect on how listening in a nonjudgmental manner can help people grow in faith. How do you listen to the people in your class? How can you help them listen to one another?

The Power of Touch

In the 1990's, the plight of children in Romanian state-run orphanages was discovered, and many of these children were adopted by families in other countries. Through a combination of political and social conditions in Romania, these children had been neglected. Even in cleaner orphanages with more staff, there was no bonding with the children, no physical contact, and no holding. Babies were swaddled, with a bottle propped in their mouths.

Studies with the adopted children revealed that all of them were developmentally delayed when they arrived in their adoptive families. The children's actions did not indicate brain damage or emotional illness; they indicated adaptations made because of the conditions of the orphanages. These children, deprived of human touch and attention, lacked communication skills, rocked back and forth or stared at their hands, and were indiscriminately friendly with any adults who paid attention to them.

After these children had lived with families in Canada and the United States for more than a year, their immediate physical and medical needs were met, but they still had social and behavioral problems. These children are amazingly resilient, and many are now developmentally comparable to their peers; but the lack of human touch and attention had a severe impact on their lives.

Human touch is important throughout the life span. Older people living alone or in nursing homes report deep longing for a loving touch and "someone who calls my name." Let us not forget that one punishment reserved for serious criminals and enemy soldiers is solitary confinement.

Appropriate or Inappropriate?

Teachers of children, youth, and adults must be aware of the power of touch—and the serious nature of abusing this power. Touching other people in appropriate ways contributes to their well-being and enhances learning. However, punitive and sexual touching can be emotionally, physically, and spiritually damaging to people.

Teachers need to think about the way we welcome, interact with, and say good-bye to students. A handshake is appropriate, but a pat on the arm (for an older person) or a pat on the head (for a child) can be either welcoming or demeaning. The recipient of your touch determines whether the touch is affirming or abusive, no matter what your intentions. It is wise to ask if a touch is OK before you do anything other than shake hands.

Spiritual Exercise

Read Luke 8:43-48. Reflect on the power of touch.

The Power of Words

The church has long known the power of words. When we pray the Lord's Prayer or sing a hymn, we are doing more than simple recitation. What we say over and over again gets in our bones and our souls and influences what we believe and how we act.

Words can build people up or demean people. Teachers need to be aware of the power of words—both the words they speak and the words students speak in their class. Affirming words, sarcasm, friendly words, and teasing words each influence a life for good or destroy self-esteem.

If we constantly criticize someone, that person will begin to believe that he or she is not a capable individual. If children are told they are fat, or dumb, or clumsy, they will have difficulty developing healthy self-esteem.

Humor Can Hurt or Heal

Humor, when used appropriately, can relieve tension and create a helpful environment for dealing with difficult topics or tasks. However, humor can also be used in a cruel manner. Jokes that belittle another group reinforce old stereotypes and contribute to an "us versus them" mentality.

Teasing can be painful for the person being teased. Even if the person laughs and appears to be unaffected, that doesn't mean that no harm has been done.

As a teacher you have a responsibility to ensure that no members of your class are being teased by other members.

Things to Consider

Ask yourself these questions as you think about what you and others say in your class.

- Do I or other class members ever engage in put-downs?
- Do I affirm class members when they offer an idea to a class?
- What do the words I use to describe God say about my understanding of God?
- Do I say things that may exclude some members of the class, for example, telling children to ask their mom something, when some children in the class may not live with their mother; or talking as if everyone in the adult class has a spouse, when some people in the class are single?
- How skilled is my class at discussing differing points of view while still respecting individuals?
- What spoken and unspoken agreements does the class have about what can or cannot be discussed?
- Does my language indicate that everyone in the class is equally valuable? For example, do I ever suggest that quiet activities are more appropriate for girls and that boys should participate more actively?
- What things are said regularly in the class that remind class members that they are beloved children of God?

Spiritual Exercise

Read John 1:1-3 slowly and meditatively. Scan Genesis, Chapter 1. Reflect upon the power of words.

Going Further

In addition to doing no harm and doing good, there is one more General Rule. In Wesley's day this was worded, "Attend to the ordinances of God." Like doing no harm and doing good, the ordinances of God are means of grace, or ways that God has provided for us to experience God's grace. They include public worship, Bible study, Holy Communion, prayer, Christian conversation, and fasting or abstinence.

Some of these are probably familiar to you and a part of your spiritual life. Others may be less familiar. As you seek to live the faith, you may want to explore some of these spiritual disciplines.

One way to be intentional about living the faith is to participate in an accountability group such as a Covenant Discipleship Group. A Covenant Discipleship Group is a small group that develops a covenant or an agreement that describes what the members intend to do to grow as disciples.

The covenant is based on the General Rule of Discipleship, a contemporary interpretation of the General Rules: "To witness to Jesus Christ in the world, and to follow his teaching through acts of compassion, justice, worship, and devotion, under the guidance of the Holy Spirit." Whether you become part of a Covenant Discipleship Group or find other ways to grow as a disciple, this statement provides an excellent guide for living out the faith.

Helpful Resources

Websites

General Board of Discipleship of The United Methodist Church (www.gbod.org). On this site you will find articles related to discipleship, teaching, and Covenant Discipleship Groups. Particular sites of interest are www.gbod.org/education and www.gbod.org/keepingintouch.

Discipleship Resources (www.discipleshipresources.org). In this online bookstore you can purchase additional copies of this booklet, other booklets in the series, and other books published by Discipleship Resources.

Books

Accountable Discipleship: Living in God's Household, by Steven W. Manskar (Discipleship Resources, 2000). Examines ways that Christians today can become accountable disciples. Based on Wesley's understanding of grace and the General Rules.

Keeping in Touch: Christian Formation and Teaching, by Carol F. Krau (Discipleship Resources, 1999). Looks at the role of the teacher in creating faith-forming classrooms.

Out of the Basement: A Holistic Approach to Children's Ministry, by Diane C. Olson (Discipleship Resources, 2001). Looks at the systems needed to create a healthy church environment for children.

Safe Sanctuaries: Reducing the Risk of Child Abuse in the Church, by Joy Thornburg Melton (Discipleship Resources, 1998). Helps congregations develop policies and procedures to ensure a safe church environment.

Ordering Information

Resources published by Discipleship Resources may be ordered online at www.discipleshipresources.org; by phone at 800-685-4370; by fax at 770-442-9742; or by mail from Discipleship Resources Distribution Center, P.O. Box 1616, Alpharetta, GA 30009-1616.